Katharina Dellbrügge

The Critical Period Hypothesis

Support and Challenge form encounters with Fera

Katharina Dellbrügge

The Critical Period Hypothesis

Support and Challenge form encounters with Feral Children

GRIN Verlag

Bibliografische Information der Deutschen Nationalbibliothek: Die Deutsche Bibliothek
verzeichnet diese Publikation in der Deutschen Nationalbibliografie; detaillierte bibliografische Daten sind im Internet über http://dnb.d-nb.de/ abrufbar.

1. Auflage 2008
Copyright © 2008 GRIN Verlag
http://www.grin.com/
Druck und Bindung: Books on Demand GmbH, Norderstedt Germany
ISBN 978-3-640-54589-6

Universität zu Köln

Hauptseminar: The Acquisition of English

SS 2008

12.09.08

The Critical Period Hypothesis

Support and Challenge form encounters with Feral Children

Table of contents

1. Introduction

Encounters with feral children have been attracting intellectual examination and curiosity since the early seventeenth century. Among others, Anthropologists, Psychologists and Linguists hoped to find answers to central questions of mankind: What makes us human beings? What distinguishes us from animals? Nature or nurture, what has greater impact on us? Do we possess innate ideas or do we need society to become human? As feral children seemed to promise answers to such existential concerns, they "have had a privileged role as objects of knowledge in Western human science" (Benzaquén 2002: 65).

The concept of the human subdivision *homo ferus* was brought up by Carl Linnè (also known as Linnaeus) in 1758. It was initially used to describe individuals who had lived in the wilderness on their own or maybe with animals. The anthropologist Robert Zingg (1940) used the translated version *feral man* in his account of "extreme cases of isolation". Shortly afterwards, the term was especially associated with children and recently also children who experienced isolation and deprivation are included in that category. So the "wildness" nowadays rather signifies a kind of strangeness or development in abnormal circumstances in general (cp. Benzaquén 2002: 66) and as such it is used in this term paper.

One field of investigation in which these case studies are frequently cited, is that of linguistics. Especially with respect to the assumption of maturational constraints on language acquisition, scholars tried to draw conclusions from the success or failure feral children exhibited after discovery. Respectively, they were interpreted as evidence or counter-evidence for the Critical Period Hypothesis (CPH) which postulates that language can only be acquired normally up to a certain age. Eric H. Lenneberg is closely connected to this assumption and it is remarkable that he did not included cases of feral children. He explicitly comments on that when he points out that such cases should not be taken as evidence because "the nature of the social and physical environment is never clear and the possibility of genetic deficiencies or congenital abnormalities can never be ruled out" (1967: 141).

Arguing in a similar fashion, Wayne Dennis (1941: 432) suggests "that these cases not be cited as evidence for any social or psychological theory". Nevertheless, they have been taken into account in the context of the CPH because many scholars think

that they offer valuable insights into the topic. This term paper attempts to clarify up to which extend they really do so.

To achieve this task, the paper is organised as follows. In Section 2 a general description of critical periods is given before turning to Lenneberg's hypothesis. Section 3 focuses on two cases that are often taken as evidence for the CPH, namely Victor and Genie. Both didn't master language acquisition to a satisfactory level. Section 4, on the other hand, deals with three children who are expounded as counter-evidence for the CPH because they caught up quickly on language learning close to age seven. In both sections, after a short description of the individual experiences prior to discovery, a detailed account of linguistic achievements and shortcomings is presented. Section 5 will discuss the outcomes and put them into a broader scientific context by adding results of further research. Section 6 offers a preliminary conclusion, namely that cases of feral children should be included as indirect evidence but that this needs to be done carefully.

2. The Critical Period Hypothesis

2.1 About critical periods

Originally the term *critical period* emerged in the field of experimental embryology. Here it was used to describe time spans in which normal embryonic development (e.g. of minnow eggs) could be inhibited or even mutated (Stockard 1978 presented in Herschensohn 2007: 7). Later on, the term also occurred in the area of animal behaviour. A famous example is Konrad Lorenz's experiment with a greylag gosling. He demonstrated that the young goose attached to the first large, moving object being around. This so-called *imprinting* occurs in the first week after hatching and turned out to be irreversible, i.e. the gosling always preferred a human, the original imprint-target, to another bird (cp. Lorenz 1937: 264). There are other interesting examples for the study of critical periods in animals including, for instance, the development of vision in kitten, the learning of birdsong or the establishment of dialectic communication systems in orca whales. Yet, for the purpose of this paper it is more significant to define critical periods as such. A single clear-cut definition,

however, is not available because the term has not been used consistently in the scientific literature.

With respect to etymology, the expression "critical" in this sense derives from the Greek words *krino* (to decide) and *krisis*, meaning "a decisive turning-point in any matter" (The Encyclopaedic Dictionary 1889: 570). In some way, during critical periods indeed decisions are made and they cannot be repeated or changed afterwards. Corresponding to that, Scott (1978) gives the following definition for them:

> The time of most rapid organization in a particular process is not only a critical period for decisions but is also an optimal period for producing desirable (or at least desired) changes in organization. Change cannot be produced before the organizational process begins nor after it has ceased. (Scott 1978: 359)

In other words, there occurs a phase of high susceptibility to certain stimuli which in return produces changes in the living system. Before and after this phase no or at least fewer susceptibility is given. These phases coincide with a developmental stage of the organism, i.e. with a certain age. Not in all, but in most cases, such a "peak period of plasticity" can be observed during stages of early development (cp. Newport et al. 2001: 482).

At first glance it might occur unpractical and risky that animals, including humans, are equipped with mechanisms which rely on such a restricted timing. According to Pinker (1994: 293) this impression arises because "most of us have an incorrect understanding of the biology of organisms' life histories". With reference to the example of metamorphosis in insects, he emphasises that "designs hang around during the times of life that they are useful, not before or after" (ibid.:294). Furthermore, Bruer (1999: 107) regards critical periods as "adaptive, clever, and efficient feats of biological engineering". For him, they "make evolutionary sense because they rely on stimuli that are ubiquitous within normal human environments" (ibid.: 110) and the same holds for animalistic environments. During critical periods, our brain seems to expect certain input and also needs it to fine-tune its neural circuits, a fact that is called *experience-expectant brain plasticity* (cp. Greenough quoted in Bruer 1999: 108). Abnormal circumstances, like deprivation, therefore make a normal development impossible because the required input does not occur.

To characterise critical periods per se, scientists hold on to some parameters that have been declared to be structurally representative for them. According to Bornstein (1987: 5), there are five of these factors[1] and the following table displays them with the corresponding examples from birdsong learning (content of this table cp. Herschensohn 2007: 11):

Parameter	Birdsong Learning
1.) onset	convergence of puberty & seasonal change
2.) terminus	completion of the learned repertoire
3.) intrinsic maturation event	hormonal change
4.) extrinsic trigger	ambient birdsong & daylight hours
5.) organismic system affected	neural architecture & sensorimotor circuits linked to song-memory

Another term that appears often in this context is "sensitive period". While critical periods were supposed to end abruptly, these periods were thought to end gradually. This distinction turned out to be useless because scientists discovered that most critical periods end gradually (cp. Bruer 1999: 104; Newport et al. 2001: 482). Nowadays both terms are used quite interchangeably.

2.2 Assuming a critical period for human language

The ultimate strength and appeal of the assumption that there must be an age sensitivity for language acquisition lies in its link to everyday experience: While observing a young child learning his/her native tongue with no apparent effort, without special grammatical instructions and in a short period of time, probably everyone starts wondering why learning a second language later in life is that much harder. Adults are able to master a second language up to a native-like level, but only as a result of a long-lasting and labour-intensive learning process. The perfect pro-

---

[1] More accurately, Bornstein declares these five parameters as rather outdated and presents seventeen features which are used recently. However, for the purpose of my term paper the "old" five are illustrating enough and are still the core of the extended register.

nunciation of a foreign language, however, is hardly ever reached. A famous example is the German-born Henry Kissinger: he retained his accent while his younger brother does not have one (cp. Pinker 1994: 291). A similar discrepancy can be seen in the case of bilingualism. For example, in immigrant families the children become native speakers of the second language while their parents will keep their foreign accents and will make more grammatical mistakes (cp. Herschensohn 2007: 2).

All in all, it seems to be a kind of folk wisdom that we (or more accurately our brains) are equipped with the necessary tools to learn our native tongue naturally at a young age, but that this ability gets lost as we grow older. At first sight that seems to be a well-understandable and logical presumption. Nonetheless, in many scientific fields (as in linguistics, neurology and biology, just to name a few) this idea of a connecting between language and maturation has been hotly debated ever since it was brought up.

Back in the 1950s this matter was not an important issue yet. As behaviourism and structuralism were dominant perspectives, the explanation for the folk belief presented above had been: language is the outcome of mechanisms like conditioning, association, practice in exercising skills and reinforcement. As B.F. Skinner puts it, "verbal behavior" is acquired by a child "when relatively unpatterned vocalizations, selectively reinforced, gradually assume forms which produce appropriate consequences in a given verbal community" (1957:31).

The dominance of the behaviourist approach declined as experimental work headed into another direction and as perspectives shifted to a biological understanding of human language. The notion of localization, for example, had a revival and the notion of a "Language Acquisition Device" came up (cp. Strozer 1994: 135). Eric H. Lenneberg, probably inspired by these tendencies, examined language as a natural phenomenon, assuming that it can be studied in a similar fashion like other aspects of human biology, e.g. anatomy. In his book B*iological Foundations of Language* (1967:374ff) he argues that

    a. **language is innately determined** (this supports Noam Chomsky's proposal of an innate Universal Grammar and is an explanation for the regularity of onset and universal pattern of language development between the second and third year of life)

5

b. **exposure to language is necessary to trigger the development of neurological language processes** (he brings up the analogy to the relationship between nourishment and growth: food is the architectural raw material which must be chemically processed before it may enter the synthesis that produces tissues and organs)

c. **first language acquisition is only successful if the learner is older than two and has not reached puberty yet** (according to him, it is impossible before age two due to maturational factors and after puberty because of the loss of "cerebral plasticity", i.e. lateralization of the brain already took place)

These three postulations are the core of the so-called *Critical Period Hypothesis (CPH)*, a meanwhile common expression in scientific publications which is attributed to Lenneberg although he did not introduce this term himself. In correspondence to Bornstein's parameters, the following illustration of Lenneberg's theory can be given (cp. Herschensohn 2007: 213):

Parameter	Language Learning
1.) onset	maturational stage at age two
2.) terminus	acquisition of a first language (possible until age twelve)
3.) intrinsic maturation event	functional specializing of the hemispheres (lateralization)
4.) extrinsic trigger	exposure to human language
5.) organismic system affected	neuromuscular system

To argue for his point of view, Lenneberg primarily used three types of evidence. Firstly, he describes cases of damaged left hemispheres which caused aphasia. These cases show that children are more likely to recover from cerebral trauma and impaired language functions than adults do (Lenneberg 1967: 142ff). A child at the age of two will struggle with the impairment in the beginning, "but soon he will start again on the road toward language acquisition, [...] until perfect speech is achieved" (ibid.: 150). Children older than two and younger than ten still have good chances for recovery, but "by the time of puberty, a turning point is reached" (ibid.).

As a second kind of evidence, he refers to language development in mentally retarded individuals. Down's syndrome children appear to follow a normal but slower course of language acquisition which ends at puberty (Lenneberg 1967:154ff). While they eventually develop language, other cognitive areas do not improve. This supports Lenneberg's assumption that language and other cognitive attributes are separated devices. Thirdly, he presents neurological studies which indicate that numerous maturational processes of the brain reach a stable (or plateau) state during the early teens (Lenneberg 1967: 162ff).

3. Two cases that seem to support the CPH

3.1 Victor

Case History

Victor,[2] also called the wild boy of Aveyron, apparently had been living in the forest for several years. First sighted in 1797, he was assumed to be approximately eleven years old. In the following year woodsmen caught the boy and brought him to the village of Lacaune (cp. Lane 1976: 6ff). He resisted violently and managed to flee back into the woods shortly afterwards. After being captured a second time he still refused to stay in the community and wandered off again (ibid.). In January 1800, probably because of hunger, he walked into the house of a dyer. Later on, the commissioner for the canton of Saint-Senin took charge of the child and sent him to an orphanage (ibid.: 9). The boy's origin could not be clarified.

After discovery

At the orphanage in Saint-Affrique his behaviour was observed as follows: he only ate potatoes and nuts and refused any kind of other food, he was constantly seeking for a way to escape, he hated clothing and he never spoke (cp. one of the administrators of the orphanage quoted in Lane 1976: 10). The only sounds he made were indistinct cries and laughter (ibid.). Apart from being subject to numerous

---

[2] This name was given to the boy by his teacher Jean Itard because he reacted strongly to the sound „o" (cp. Lane 1976:112)

newspaper headlines and common curiosity, Victor soon attracted the attention of scholars who were interested in the nature of mankind.

The first who was able to examine him was Abbé Pierre-Joseph Bonnaterre, a professor of natural history. A detailed account of his observations was published in 1800. According to this treatise, Victor's outer appearance and body shape was normal, apart from numerous scars (Bonnaterre in Lane 1976: 33ff). Taken for deaf at the beginning, his senses turned out to be good. However, his sense of hearing seemed to be very specialised in an usual way: When being talked to, he didn't show any reactions, but when a walnut was cracked behind him he turned to glance at his favourite food (ibid.: 39). Moreover, his senses of smell and taste were of primary importance: he examined a lot with his nose (ibid.: 36) and was constantly looking for something to eat (ibid.: 39). Affection or fondness of another person was always linked to the satisfaction of his needs or his desire for food. The few gestures he used where also related to that purpose of satisfaction (ibid.: 37).

Concerning his voice organs Bonnaterre notes that Victor's tongue was flexible and intact but there was a long scar on the glottis and the wound might have caused Victor's speechlessness (ibid.: 37ff). There was no obvious indication for retardation (ibid.: 42), but Bonnaterre concluded that Victor "is truly and purely an animal" and that "enormous barriers separate him" from other, civilized human beings (ibid.: 48).

In the summer of 1800 Victor was taken to the Institute for Deaf-Mutes in Paris. Many scholars came to see him and tried different methods to instruct him (ibid.: 53). All of them failed and the diagnosis of congenital idiocy was put forward. Nevertheless, the young physician Jean Itard took up his attempts to train the boy. For the next six years he spent a lot of time with him and tried to teach Victor how to use language, a capacity which he thought to be existent and which only needed to be activated (cp. Blumenthal 2003: 138). Inspired by the work of the French philosopher Condillac, he put the main focus on Victor's senses, "the portals of the mind" (Lane 1976:101). After providing a stable and harmonic environment, he began the instructions. As Victor didn't show any reactions to heat and cold, Itard arranged different exercises, e.g. daily hot baths (ibid.: 102). After three month Victor had developed a sensibility for temperature. Furthermore, he started to show affection for other people, especially for the woman he lived with, Madame Guérin (ibid.: 110).

Advancements in the area of speech were more difficult. Itard was sure that Victor's voice organs were intact and that the scar over the glottis came from a rather superficial wound (ibid.: 112). The first correctly pronounced word Victor uttered was *lait* (milk), so apparently he had some basic vocal imitation skills (ibid.: 113). However, he never used this word to formulate a request, he only used it for naming, i.e. he said it after he had received the milk. Altogether, his vocal skills included five vowels and four consonants (ibid.: 114). To articulate his needs, he still used gestures and all of them were closely linked to objects or were the simulations of actions one could perform with these objects (cp. ibid.: 115ff).

In a next phase of instruction, Itard tried to teach Victor the connection between pictures and objects. He drew simple sketches on a blackboard, made the relationship to the corresponding object clear and asked Victor to bring him one of the objects by pointing to a picture (cp. ibid.: 117ff). This procedure only worked to a certain degree and it was easy to distract or frustrate Victor. Itard continued with other matching tasks. Later on, he also included letters and written words. Like that Victor learned many nouns, verbs and adjectives which he could use correctly in small sentences (cp ibid.: 147ff). He produced these sentences via metal letters or printed cards. So Itard decided to teach Victor how to write and the boy made progress in learning the basics of this skill. However, the attempt to teach him how to speak failed (ibid.: 153). The onset of puberty and sexual desires made the training even more complicated and finally, in 1806, Itard ended the instructions. Victor lived with Madame Guérin until he died in 1828.

3.2. Genie

Case History

The case of Genie[3] is often regarded as a modern counterpart to Victor although the similarities are rather few. The wilderness that Genie encountered was not one of the woods and fields, but that of her father. After he was convinced that his daughter, born in April 1957, was mentally retarded he began to lock her up in a small room with closed curtains and hardly any furniture. There the 20-month old child was tied to

---

[3] This name was given to her by Curtiss et al. to protect her privacy and identity. It was chosen because it reflects that the girl "emerged into human society past childhood, having existed previously as something other than fully human" (Curtiss 1977:xiii).

a potty chair most of the time, unable to move (Curtiss 1977: 5). If she made any noise, her father would beat her with a wooden stick (ibid.: 6). He never talked with her, but made dog-like sounds (ibid.). Genie's mother was frightened of her violent husband and an increasing blindness made it impossible to care for her daughter properly. Therefore Genie's older brother became her main caretaker but he only barked or growled at her, too (ibid.). Genie was fed only on cereals, baby food or soft-boiled eggs (ibid.). She didn't experience much tactile or visual stimulation or any sounds because the father neither allowed loud conversations nor a radio or TV.

Like that the family lived for several years. However, in 1970 the mother fled together with her daughter (ibid.: 7). Shortly afterwards they went to the family aids to apply financial support. There the extremely thin and small girl alerted the employers and made them call the police. Genie was admitted to a hospital and her parents were charged. The father committed suicide on the day of the trial.

After Discovery

Genie had great difficulties to walk, did not know how to chew solid food, did not show any emotions, did not speak and wasn't sensible to temperature. The only sounds she produced were a few words and a whimper (cp. Curtiss 1977: 9). When she became very upset, she got a tantrum, i.e. she would scratch or hurt herself, blow her nose into clothes and would spit. During such times, however, there was no vocalization at all (ibid.: 10).

Specially designed comprehension tasks showed that she had hardly any understanding of grammatical structures (cp. Fromkin et al. 1974: 593). Therefore, at the age of 13 years and seven months, "she was faced with the task of first-language acquisition, a task normally completed before age five" (Curtiss et al. 1974: 530). The scholar's main question was whether Genie would be able to "catch up" (Fromkin et al. 1974: 589) and whether she would be able to learn language with the help of professional instruction.

Eight months after Genie had been found she started to utter word sequences containing two words (cp. ibid.: 596). The structures of these two-word strings were either *Modifier + Noun* (e.g. "more soup") or genitive constructions realized via *Noun + Noun* (e.g. "Genie purse"). Shortly afterwards verb phrases followed: subject-N + V

10

(e.g. "Curtiss cough") and V + object-N (e.g. "want milk"). She also uttered sentences with a noun and a predicate adjective (e.g. "Dave sick").

When she started to produce three- and four-word sentences in November 1971, like "Tori chew glove" or "little white clear box", the scientists concluded that "syntactic relations which were only assumed to be present in her two-word utterances were now overtly expressed" (Fromkin et al. 1974: 596). While many of Genie's sentences did not cover subjects before, the three- and four-word sentences included both subjects and objects. Genie also showed recursive syntactic operations at this stage, i.e. she inserted whole utterances from her two-word stage as constituents into the longer strings during the later stages (ibid.).

Three months later, Genie made her first negative statements but she kept inserting the negative markers "no" and "not" at the beginning of the sentence instead of inserting it inside the sentence (Curtiss 1977: 150) Finally, by the end of 1974, she performed negative movement transformations and produced sentences with internal negation (ibid.: 151). The dummy DO occurred a few months later to form negative statements but not on other occasions (ibid.:175). Genie also began to produce locative nouns (e.g. "play gym"). Complex VPs were first used in July 1972 (e.g. "want go shopping"). By 1974, Genie had also begun to use the morpheme "ing" to describe ongoing action and she used other morphemes like plural "s" and possessive "s" (Fromkin et al.: 597). For the latter case she also used constructions with the verb "have". Determiners, prepositions and imperatives had entered her speech, too (cp. Curtiss 1977: 146ff).

One of Genie's greatest achievements was the use of recursive compound NPs, observed from December 1971 onwards: She would "connect" two notions by a recursive operation ("cat dog hurt") while she only referred to one entity at a time beforehand, saying things like "cat hurt" or "dog hurt" (Fromkin et al. 1974: 597). So Genie was able to construct new combinations out of linguistic elements available to her and she conjoined sentences, "two essential elements of language that permit the generation of an infinite set of sentences" (ibid.)

By 1974, many aspects of Genie's linguistic knowledge paralleled that of two-and-a-half-year old children (ibid.: 598). Her vocabulary, though, was cognitively more sophisticated and larger as one would assume at that stage: She used colour words and numbers which usually enter a child's vocabulary much later and when she

began to produce two-word utterances, she possessed an active vocabulary of about 200 words, while 50 would be the normal size for children at this stage (ibid.: 599). Moreover, Genie could understand all the WH-question words and differentiations such as comparative and superlative or "more" and "less" (ibid.).

These findings indicated that Genie's cognitive development was faster than her linguistic development. Tests of her metal age proofed that. For example, on the Vineland Social Maturity Scale, her first score had been about 15 months, seven months later she scored 42 months (ibid.). A similar discrepancy in achievement could be observed in Genie's comprehension and production of language. She was able to understand most of the basic English structures, but not all of these were reflected in her speech (Curtiss 1977: 209).

Least successful was Genie's development when it came to speech production and phonology. She was not able to control her vocal organs because she had learnt to suppress the production of sounds instead of learning the necessary neuromuscular control (Fromkin et al. 1974: 594). She had great difficulties in adjusting air volume and flow, as well as glottal structures and vibrations (Curtiss et al. 1974: 532). Her speech stayed telegraphic and monotonic.

4. Two cases that seem to question the CPH

4.1 Isabelle

Case History

This case of severe deprivation actually started with the preceding generation. Isabelle's mother[4] was a deaf, mute and uneducated woman who had lost the sight of her right eye due to an accident in early childhood (Mason 1942: 295). The fact that she didn't begin to speak was thought to be the result of a lesion in Broca's area, also due to the accident. Later on, this diagnosis turned out to be wrong: the accident caused deafness and she could have been educated in an appropriate school (ibid.: 298). She communicated with her family via some simple, self-invented gestures, spent the days doing simple kind of housework and wasn't allowed to leave the house by herself (ibid.: 295). Therefore it came as a surprise when her family found out that

---

[4] The name *Isabelle* is fictitious.

she had somehow become pregnant. Apparently the family could not stand the existence of an illegitimate child. During pregnancy and for six and a half years after Isabelle's birth in April 1932, mother and child were kept in a dark room.

Due to the lack of sunshine and fresh air and inadequacy of diet, Isabelle became rachitic. Her legs grew in such a twisted way that she wasn't able to walk properly. The only person Isabelle had contact to during that period of imprisonment was her mute mother. They used gestures to communicate with each other. Finally, Isabelle's mother managed to escape with her daughter in November 1938.

After discovery

Isabelle was taken to a children's hospital on the 16th of November 1938 for orthopaedic surgery and physiotherapy. At that time she was thought to be mute, too. The only way of expressing herself was a set of gestures which were similar to sign language used by deaf children (Mason 1942: 299). Her performance on psychological tests equalled that of three years-old whereas any test involving linguistic abilities failed (ibid.: 298). That led to the assumption that she might be mentally retarded. Towards strangers she reacted fearful or even hostile. Marie K. Mason, her speech therapist, describes in detail how delicate it was to gain Isabelle's confidence. She decided to educate the girl via the use of "gesture, facial expression, pantomime, dramatization and imitation" (ibid.: 299).

Already one week after Mason's first visit, Isabelle made attempts of vocalization, i.e. imitative utterances like [ba] for 'ball' and [a:] for 'car' (ibid.: 299). After repeating these words several times, they "were correctly spoken and became for her the verbal symbols of the objects represented" (ibid). The first step towards a rapid linguistic improvement was taken.

After two months her vocabulary (mainly consisting of nouns and verbs) had grown rapidly and she could distinguish yellow from other colours. Within three months she uttered simple sentences voluntarily, like "I love my baby" and "Close your eyes" (ibid.: 301). After four months she commenced to identify written words like 'blue' and 'cat' and got formal lessons to learn how to read and write (ibid.: 302). After one year of training she was able to write nicely, to comprehend numbers up to 20, to listen carefully while a story is read aloud and to join rhythmic activities (ibid.: 302ff).

Sometimes her mental processes seemed to outperform her ability of correct articulation and thus, an utterance resulted in jabbering (ibid.: 302).

As another six months had gone by, Isabelle possessed a vocabulary of 1500 to 2000 words, could retell stories or made up her own. She also formulated intelligent and full-length questions like "Does your dog sleep in your bed?" and "Why does the paste come out if one upsets the jar?" (ibid.: 303). At the age of eight years she was considered to be a child of normal intelligence (ibid.: 304) and at the point of last account at the age of about 14 years she had been well established at a normal public school (cp. Davis 1947: 437).

All in all, Isabelle went through the typical developmental stages of language learning but at a greatly accelerated pace, i.e. she covered in twenty-two month the stages of language acquisition that are normally distributed over a period of six years (Davis 1947: 436). This success was probably due to the prolonged and highly skilled speech training, excellent medical care and the effects of social interactions in an enriched environment.

4.2 P.M. and J.M – The Czech twins

Case History

The boys P.M and J.M., also often called the Koluchová twins named after Jarmila Koluchová who studied them intensively, were born as monozygotic twins on the 4th of September 1960 in Czechoslovakia. Their mother died soon after giving birth and they spent their first eleven months in a children's home. Documents from this period showed that their physical and mental development had been normal (Koluchová 1972:107). After another six months with a maternal aunt they were brought back to their father who had married a second time. The stepmother was a woman of "average intelligence, but egocentric" (ibid.: 108) and commonly described as cool and aggressive. Altogether, after marriage she had to take care for six children: two natural elder sisters of the twins, the boys themselves and two children of her own. She never acknowledged the twins as her children and her "disinterest developed into active hostility" towards them (ibid.).

The outcome was that the boys had to live isolated and under inhuman conditions for the next five and a half years. They were kept either in an empty, small and

14

unheated closet or in the cellar (ibid.). They had to sleep on a polythene sheet on the floor, were never allowed into the other rooms of the house and were grossly neglected. The Stepmother forbade other family members to talk to the twins or play with them. Furthermore, they were severely physically punished by their stepmother and their father. At large, the twins experienced a very dismissive environment. They spared any (normal) relationships and stimulation.

After Discovery

The mistreatment of the twins was discovered in December 1967 and they were removed from the family (Koluchová 1972: 108). They showed problems with walking and were afflicted with rachitis which was due to malnutrition, lack of sunshine, fresh air and exercise (ibid.). Apparently they had had no contact with otherwise familiar things such as mechanical toys, television or traffic. Confronted with these they showed reactions of surprise or even fright (ibid.: 109). The meaning of pictures was unclear to them and therefore it was not possible to use them for measurements of their vocabulary (ibid.).

At the chronological age of seven years and three months (i.e. in December 1967) their overall mental age was considered to be around the three year level. Regarding their language abilities, spontaneous speech was hardly perceptible and when imitating adult speech they only repeated two or three words at a time with poor articulation (ibid.). Moreover, they seemed to understand questions but were not able to answer them. Instead of sounds they used a system of very simple, mimic gestures to communicate with each other. Therefore, "it was obvious that they were not used to speech as a means of communication" (ibid.).

The fastest recovery took place after the twins had begun to live with their foster family. Two unmarried middle-aged sisters adopted the children in July 1969 and many of the outcomes of earlier deprivation gradually declined (c.p. ibid.: 111ff). By September 1969, their mental age had increased by three years compared to the first account 15 months beforehand (ibid.: 112). They showed a readiness for schooling and were admitted to the first class in a school for mentally retarded children. One year later, it became obvious that this school didn't suit their needs and potentials. Therefore, the boys were enrolled in the second class of a normal public school. Later

on, they even managed to catch up more: they moved from the fourth directly to the sixth class (Koluchová 1976: 182).

Ever since the twins had been removed from their original family, they received professional speech training and pronunciation practice as well as special medical and psychological care (cp. ibid.: 185). By the time of writing her second report on the twins' development Koluchová observed that "their speech was entirely adequate for their age, both in form and content" (ibid.: 181). Concerning social behaviour, the boys didn't show any abnormalities either and their I.Q.s had reached an age appropriate level (cp. ibid.: 182).

5. Discussion

In both Victor and Genie language acquisition was only successful to a certain, rather low degree. Different explanations for this can be put forward: (1) they were mentally retarded from birth on, (2) their isolation caused a mental deficiency which prohibited language development and (3) they were too old, i.e. they had missed the critical period.

As to Victor, the first assumption is hard to negate because means of medical investigations were less developed in Itard's times. Scholars still discuss whether Victor was mentally retarded from birth on or not. Some, like Bettelheim (1959), suggest that he was an autistic child but that this kind of retardation was unknown in the beginning of the 19th century. The second hypothesis, i.e. the possibility that prolonged isolation and lack of human contact can cause severe deficits is often cited. Rauber ([1885] in Blumenthal 2003) introduced the term *dementia ex separatione* to describe this disorder. Similar to that Lane (1976: 179) supports the assumption, that Victor was not autistic, although he showed several features of autism, but that his symptoms "are the result of his isolation in the wild". Despite the mental deficits one assumes, the fact remains that Victor managed to survive on his own for a long time, an achievement probably not reachable for a severely handicapped child.

Regarding the third explanation, Itard himself noted that for Victor's acquisition of speech "much more time and much more trouble will be necessary than would be

required for the least gifted of infants" (quoted in Lane 1976: 180). In the end he concluded that age had been a limiting factor for his education of Victor because the "imitative force [...], which is very energetic and active during the first years of his life, wanes rapidly with age" (ibid.: 129).

According to the scientist who studied Genie, a mental retardation from birth on did not exist. They stated that "from the meagre medical records at our disposal, then, there is no indication of early retardation" (Fromkin et al. 1974: 591). The skull was normally developed, no metabolic disorders, neurological diseases or chromosomal abnormalities were discovered. Although she was functionally retarded and emotionally disturbed, she did not seem to be autistic. Furthermore, Genie's mother reported that Genie had begun to formulate words prior to her confinement but stopped shortly afterwards (Curtiss 1977: 208). A mentally retarded child of 20 months would not start to talk at this age. Therefore, the scientist supported the second hypothesis mentioned above to account for Genie's condition: They suggested that it was caused by the "intensity and duration of her psychosocial and physical deprivation" (ibid.: 592).

As regards the CPH, Curtiss (1977: 208) emphasizes that Genie is a "test case" because she did not have adequate linguistic input during the period from age two to puberty. Curtiss argues that a "strong version" of Lennberg's hypothesis, claiming that natural language acquisition cannot occur after puberty at all, could be disproved because Genie did develop language slowly but steadily (cp. 1977: 209). The question remains whether Genie's accomplishments really are a kind of natural language. Chomsky, for example, states, that her knowledge of language is different because it probably "does not involve the normal computational system of language", but only a "conceptual system" which can be regarded as rather "primitive" (Chomsky 1980: 57).

Curtiss mentions further, that a "weak version", indicating that natural language acquisition cannot develop *normally* after puberty, could not be disproved because Genie's language exhibited common features of abnormal language development: in addition to the disparity between comprehension and production, Genie showed a high variability in rule application, stereotypic speech, a retarded rate of development and a failure to acquire certain syntactic entities (cp. ibid.: 209ff). Moreover, Genie's development was mainly the result of professional therapy and training while normal

17

children do not require such explicit instruction and start learning a language spontaneously.

Another interesting discovery was Genie's right-hemisphere dominance for language which was established due to Dichotic Listening Tests, Tachistoscopic Tests and evoked potential studies. In fact, her right hemisphere seemed to be responsible for all mental functioning, including language and non-language processing, "thus Genie is not merely one of those individuals with 'reversed' laterality" (Krashen 1973: 71). These findings seem to support the assumption that the left hemisphere must be stimulated during a certain period of time because afterwards it may no longer be able to specialize for language[5] (cp Krashen 1973: 72), leaving most of the control to the right hemisphere (cp. Curtiss 1977: 234). While Lenneberg marked the end of lateralization at puberty, Krashen marks the end at age five (1973: 72).

Genie being a "right-hemisphere functioner" (Curtiss, 1977: 234) also corresponds to Knudsen's description of sensitive periods in neural pathways. He states for cases of deprivation, that "circuits acquire highly abnormal patterns of connectivity" which is probably due to the fact that these circuits are "never activated strongly by experience" (2004: 1420). Unfortunately Curtiss fails to present evidence which unquestionable confirm that Genie's left hemisphere was neither abnormal nor defective.

Additionally, there is another presumption which is strengthened by Genie's language development. Namely, that a critical period exists only for some elements of language; a view adopted by many scholars. Lederberg and Spencer (2005: 142ff), for example, draw the following conclusions after evaluating their study with deaf individuals: age of exposure seems to affect lexical growth rate (i.e. young learners acquire more words faster) and there appears to be age-constraints "for ultimate attainment of efficient and automatic semantic processing". Newport (2002: 738) remarks in a similar fashion that "critical period effects thus appear to focus on formal properties of language (phonology, morphology and syntax) and not the processing of meaning". In fact, it would have been surprising if such a complex phenomenon as language could be reduced to a single critical period. As Hurford mentions, the critical

---

[5] This attribution of functions corresponds mainly to right-handed individuals. Genie appeared to be right-handed.

period in this case has to be multilayered, "just as the object acquired - a language - has separate components" (1991: 161).

Genie's gaining of a large vocabulary and her failure to learn complex grammatical structures fit it that picture. From a grammatical point of view, she did not develop further than at a VP stage, "a level of syntactic achievement that enables sequencing of lexical items, but no use of functional categories (hence morphology)" (Herschensohn 2007: 229). Furthermore, "severe timing constraints on the development of acoustic phonological processing" can be assumed (Grimshaw et al. 1998: 241) which limit the learning of spoken but not signed language. Therefore, "one might expect that Genie would have had greater success with a signed language" (ibid.). In fact, attempts had been made to teach Genie sign language, but the results of this undertaking are not presented.

The outcome of Isabelle and the Czech twins, on the other hand, was completely diverse: They developed normally after their discovery. The factors contributing to that might be (1) they did not experience complete isolation, (2) they were placed in a socially warm and stable environment and (3) they were still young enough, i.e. they were still in the critical period.

Regarding factor one, it is noteworthy that Isabelle had her deaf mother to interact with and the twins had each other. The boys had a very close relationship, much firmer than brothers of their age generally have (Koluchová 1976:184). On top of that, they had spent some time during the first eleven months of their life in a children's home where they developed normally. Koluchová assumes that they acquired a passive knowledge of language during that "preparatory period of speech" and that they kept this knowledge in a latent form during deprivation (ibid.: 181). David Skuse (1994: 43), who compared and studied several cases of extreme deprivation, states that "interpersonal interaction" is a "necessary pre-condition" for language acquisition. The stimulation in both scenarios was not the most benefiting and educative one but at least there was some companionship given.

The second factor should not be underestimated. As to the twins, they made most rapid progress after being placed into a loving and cheerful environment (cp. Koluchová 1972: 112) and their foster-mother became "the most effective and integrative curative factor" (Koluchová 1976: 185). Victor might have experienced a similar bond to Madame Guérin, but to establish such an environment for Genie

19

completely failed. She could not build up long-lasting relationships with people because no stable environment was provided for her (cp. Benzaquén 2006: 249ff). In 1975 she went to live with her mother who could not cope with her. After that she lived in several foster homes where she was mistreated and physically abused. Today she lives sheltered accommodation for adults; apparently she has stopped speaking and lost many of the skills acquired through therapy.

Concerning the age factor, it is striking that children who overcame their negative experiences (cp. Skuse 1984), like Isabelle and the twins, were age seven and below. Apparently, as a limit "age twelve appears to be the line drawn in the sand" but so far there is not enough evidence available (Herschensohn 2007: 99). The children also had in common, that they recovered at a fast path and "the evidence suggests that if recovery of normal ability in a particular faculty is going to occur, rapid progress is the rule" (Skuse 1984: 564). This is a feature of critical periods which can be observed in other species (e.g. chaffinches): as soon as deprivation is ended and the appropriate stimulus is provided, the animals will catch up quickly (cp. Herschensohn 2007: 81). In addition to that, if one assumes that lateralization is finished at age 5 like Krashen (1973) does, Isabelle and the twins can be taken as counter-evidence for Lenneberg's supposition that language acquisition and lateralization go hand in hand.

Another explanation for the achievements of these late language learners is an extension of the critical period. Research revealed that the time span of such periods can be altered by experience. For example, isolation from the stimulus will extend it while exposition to a strongly preferred stimulus will shorten it (cp. Newport et al. 2001: 488). During isolation, animals were able to keep their sensitivity to the missing stimulus and were still able to learn after the isolation (ibid.). However, this alteration of the period only works to a certain degree and finally plasticity will decline. This might have already been the case with Genie and Victor.

6. Conclusion

Lenneberg's attempts to study language as a biological phenomenon include the concept of innateness. If we lived in a completely unethical world, we could directly test his propositions by depriving infants under controlled conditions and in experimental settings. As such experiments are not possible, "the discovery and description of innate mechanisms is a thoroughly empirical procedure" (Lenneberg 1967: 393). The problem with empirical evidences is, though, that a theory can not be proven entirely. There always remains a mist of doubt, because the only evidence available is indirect evidence. It may produce better support for a given theory, but "we cannot prove it to be true" (Chomsky 1980: 191).

The cases of feral children can be regarded as such indirect evidence. Although they do not offer final answers to the great questions of mankind as was once expected, they do provide different scientific fields with valuable indications. A problem is that they can be taken as evidence for different, even opposed theories, depending on the respective interpretations. Genie's case, for example, is mainly presented as evidence for the CPH. However, it was also produced as evidence against it, because considerable language acquisition did occur after puberty.

Due to the facts described, the inclusion of feral children in scientific work should be a careful one. Conclusions drawn from these cases can only be preliminary ones and should be sustained by evidence from other sources. If this term paper represents such a sensible handling, its task is achieved.

7. Bibliography

Bettelheim, B. (1959). Feral Children and Autistic Children. *The American Journal of Sociology* 64.5: 455-467

Benzaquén, A. (2002). John, Genie, and Kaspar: Some recent scientific uses of wildness, confinement and abuse. In: Cook, D. (ed.). *Symbolic Childhood.* New York: Peter Lang, 65-85

---. (2006). *Encounters with wild children: Temptation and Disappointment in the Study of human Nature.* Montreal: McGill-Queen's University Press

Bornstein, M. (ed.) (1987). *Sensitive Periods in Development – Interdisciplinary Perspectives.* Hillsdale: Lawrence Erlbaum Associates

Blumenthal, P.J. (2003). *Kaspar Hausers Geschwister – Auf der Suche nach dem wilden Menschen.* Wien/Frankfurt: Deuticke

Bruer, J. (1999). *The Myth of the first three Years – A new understanding of early brain development and lifelong learning.* New York: The Free Press

Chomsky, N. (1980). *Rules and Representations.* New York: Columbia University Press

"critical". *The Encyclopaedic Dictionary* (1889). Volume 4. New York: Cassell & Company

Curtiss, S. (1977). *Genie – A Psycholinguistic Study of a Modern-Day "Wild Child".* New York: Academic Press

Curtiss, S., Fromkin, V., Krashen, S., Rigler, D. & Rigler, M. (1974). The linguistic development of Genie. *Language* 50.3: 528-554

Davis, K. (1947). Final note on a case of extreme isolation. *The American Journal of Sociology* 45.4:432-437

Dennis, W. The significance of feral man. *The American Journal of Psychology* 54. 3: 425-432

Grimshaw, G., Adelstein, A., Bryden, M. & MacKinnon, G. (1998). First-language acquisition in adolescence: Evidence for a critical period for verbal language development. *Brain and Language* 63: 237-255

Herschensohn, J. (2007). *Language Development and Age.* Cambridge: Cambridge University Press

Hurford, J. (1991). The evolution of the critical period for language acquisition. *Cognition* 40: 159-201

Fromkin et al. (1974). The development of language in Genie: a case of language acquisition beyond the 'critical period'. In: Clark, V. et al. (eds.) (1998). *Language-Readings in Language and Culture.* New York: Bedford/St. Martin's, 588-605

Knudsen, E. (2004). Sensitive periods in the development of the brain and behavior. *Journal of Cognitive Neuroscience* 16.8: 1412-1425

Koluchová, J. (1972). Severe deprivation in twins: a case study. *The Journal of Child Psychology and Psychiatry* 13.2: 107-114.

---. (1976). The further development of twins after severe and prolonged deprivation: a second report. *The Journal of Child Psychology and Psychiatry* 17. 3: 181-188.

Krashen, S. (1973). Lateralization, language learning and the critical period: some new evidence. *Language and Learning* 23.1: 63–74

Lane, H. (1976). *The Wild Boy of Aveyron.* London: George Allen & Unwin Ltd.

Lederberg, A., Spencer, P. (2005). Critical Periods in the Acquisition of lexical skills – Evidence from deaf individuals. In: Fletcher, P., Miller, J. (eds.). Developmental

Theory and Language Disorders. Amsterdam: John Benjamins Publishing
    Company
Lorenz, K. (1937). The companion in the bird's world. *AuK* 54.3: 245-273
Mason, M. K. (1942). Learning to speak after six and one-half years of silence. *The
    Journal of Speech Disorders* 7.4: 295-304.
Newport, E.L. (2002). Critical periods in language development. In: Nadel, L. (ed.).
    Encyclopedia of Cognitive Science. London: Macmillan Publishers Ltd./Nature
    Publishing Group, 737-740
Newport, E., Bavelier, D., & Neville, H. (2001). Critical thinking about critical periods:
    Perspectives on a critical period for language acquisition. In: Dupoux, E. (ed.).
    *Language, Brain and Cognitive Development: Essays in Honor of Jacques
    Mehler*. Cambridge: MIT Press.
Pinker, S. (1994). *The Language Instinct – The New Science of Language and Mind*.
    London: Penguin Press
Scott, J. (ed.) (1978). *Critical Periods*. Stroudsburg: Dowden, Hutchinson & Ross
Skinner, B. (1957). *Verbal Behavior*. New York: Appleton-Century-Crofts
Skuse, D. (1984). Extreme deprivation in early childhood – II Theoretical issues and
    comparative review. In: *Journal of Child Psychology and Psychiatry* 25. 4, 543-
    572
---. (1994). Extreme deprivation in early childhood. In: Bishop, D., Mogford, K. (eds.)
    Langauge Development in Exceptional Circumstances. Hillsdale: Lawrence
    Erlbaum Associates
Strozer, J. (1994). *Language Acquisition after Puberty*. Washington, D.C.:
    Georgetown University Press
Zingg, R. (1940). Feral man and extreme cases of isolation. In: The American Journal
    of Psychology. 53.4: 487-517

Lightning Source UK Ltd.
Milton Keynes UK
UKOW02f0923020516

273369UK00001B/79/P